THE
BOVRIL
COOKBOOK

THE BOVRIL COOKBOOK

PAUL HARTLEY

ABSOLUTE PRESS

In association with
www.breakfastandbrunch.com
and
www.paulhartleyfood.com

First published in Great Britain
in 2009
by Absolute Press
Scarborough House
29 James Street West
Bath BA1 2BT England
Phone 44 (0) 1225 316013
Fax 44 (0) 1225 445836
E-mail info@absolutepress.co.uk
Web www.absolutepress.co.uk

Publisher
Jon Croft
Commissioning Editor
Meg Avent
Art Direction and Design
Matt Inwood
Design Assistant
Claire Siggery
Publishing Assistant
Andrea O' Connor
Photography
Matt Inwood
Food Stylist
Andrea O'Connor

© Absolute Press, 2009

Text copyright
© Paul Hartley, 2008
Photography copyright
© Absolute Press, 2009

A catalogue record of this book
is available from the British
Library

ISBN 9781906650025

Printed and bound by
Butler Tanner & Dennis,
Frome, England

BOVR

THE GUARANTEED F
OF PRIME OX E

DESIGNED & PRINTED BY NATHANIEL LLOYD & C? QUEEN VICTORIA S! LONDON.

RIL BO

RODUCT
EEF

THE GUA
OF F

The BOVRIL
Recipe Collection

The interesting thing about Bovril is that it evokes so many memories spanning so many generations. Writing this book afforded me the privilege of meeting a wealth of people who were almost personally protective about 'their' Bovril. Within this collection, I've fused numerous delicious flavours with Bovril and lifted those flavours to new heights. It's an indulgent and sometimes surprising collection that conveys the greatness and versatility of a wonderful extract, revealing just why Bovril has lingered on the palate for as long as it has lived in our hearts and minds. I experiment endlessly: do likewise and adapt the recipes to suit your tastes.

VENISON, BEETROOT & RED WINE CASSEROLE

A really rich winter warmer enhanced by the colour and texture of deep red beetroot.

SERVES 6

1kg diced venison
2 tablespoons seasoned flour
2–3 tablespoons vegetable oil
12 shallots
12 juniper berries
1 heaped tablespoon redcurrant jelly
350ml red wine
1 tablespoon Bovril
12 uncooked baby beetroots, peeled
300ml beef stock
2 tablespoons chopped mixed fresh thyme and parsley

Preheat the oven to 160°C/325°F/Gas 3.

Put the venison into a large bowl, sprinkle over the seasoned flour and toss it all to coat. Heat a little of the oil in a large frying pan and brown off the venison in batches without overcrowding the pan, adding more oil as required.

Transfer the meat with a slotted spoon to a casserole dish.

Heat the remaining oil in the frying pan and cook the shallots for 5 minutes. Then add the juniper berries, lightly crushed, the redcurrant jelly, red wine, Bovril, beetroot, stock and half the herbs and bring up to the boil. Pour this into the casserole dish over the venison, stir everything together and cover and cook for 2 hours.

Remove the casserole from the oven, check the seasoning, scatter with the remaining fresh herbs and serve with some delicious celeriac mash.

Staggering Stories of STRENGTH

CHEESY CHICKEN TAGLIATELLE

A delicious and filling pasta – adding Bovril really increases the depth of meaty flavour.

SERVES 2–3

3 teaspoons Bovril
300ml hot milk
50g unsalted butter
3 tablespoons olive oil
1 red onion, roughly chopped
2 cloves garlic, finely diced
1 tablespoon tomato purée
1 teaspoon mixed herbs
350g chicken breasts, cut roughly into 1.5cm chunks
100ml white wine
300g tagliatelle
salt and freshly ground black pepper
100g Parmesan, grated
fresh parsley, chopped

First, dissolve 2 teaspoons of the Bovril in the hot milk. Heat the butter and oil over a medium heat in a frying pan and add the onion, garlic, tomato purée and mixed herbs. Mix well together. When the onion begins to colour, add the chicken and cook for 10 minutes. Turn up the heat and pour in the wine and the milk with Bovril. Season well and simmer for 15 minutes or until the sauce has thickened and the chicken is well coated and tender. You may need to add a drop of water to get the right consistency for the tagliatelle sauce.

Meanwhile, bring some water to the boil in a separate pan and add the last teaspoon of Bovril. Slide in the tagliatelle and cook for 5–6 minutes or until it's *al dente*. Drain the pasta and serve in warm pasta bowls. Spoon over the chicken sauce adding grated Parmesan and a flourish of parsley.

Hard of Hearing

In 2007, so-called Ironman of Leicester, Manjit Singh, pulled off the astonishing feat of towing a seven-and-a-half-tonne aircraft nearly four metres using just clamps and rope... attached to his ears! The stunt, at East Midlands Airport in Derby, resulted in 57-year-old Singh setting a world record – he has 25 stacked against his name. It took Singh a long time to psych up for the attempt, and then ten worrying seconds of stubborn resistance before the 'Jetstream 41' passenger plane slowly started to inch forward down the runway. When he's not piling a load onto his lobes, he's busy setting or breaking other world records which involve pulling double-decker buses with his hair, doing push-ups on his fingertips and inflating weather balloons using raw lung power.

BOVRIL & RICE BREAD

You've eaten Bovril on bread, now you can try it *in* bread – it really works.

For the rice
60g rice, uncooked

For the rest of the loaf
30g unsalted butter
1 medium onion, finely chopped
500g strong plain white flour
7g active yeast (or one sachet)
1 teaspoon sea salt
1 tablespoon fresh thyme leaves
1 tablespoon Bovril dissolved in 150ml boiling water
150ml cold water

Boil the rice for 7 minutes until cooked through but not too soft. Tip into a sieve, rinse with water from a freshly boiled kettle and set aside.

While the rice is cooking, heat the butter in a small frying pan and sauté the onion until soft, but not browned. In a large bowl, combine the flour, yeast and salt, then mix in the rice, onion and thyme.

Add the cold water to the Bovril and stir into the other ingredients. It will be a little stickier than normal. Knead for 4–5 minutes (either by hand or using a freestanding mixer) adding a little extra flour if necessary. Leave to rise in a warm place until doubled in size.

Knock back the dough by gently pushing your fist into the centre and knead again for a couple of minutes. Form into a loaf and transfer to an oiled tin. Leave to prove again for about an hour until well risen.

While the loaf is on its second proving pre-heat your oven to 220°C/425°F/Gas 7. Put in the loaf and bake for 10 minutes then reduce the heat to 200°C/400°F/Gas 6 for a further 20 minutes.

The loaf is cooked if it sounds hollow when rapped on the bottom.

Opposite
In need of hot water!
c. end of 19th Century

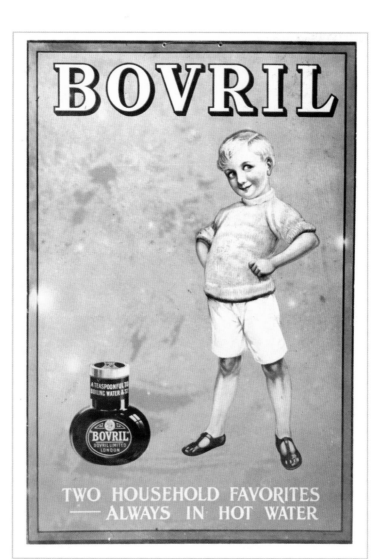

ALMOND BRITTLE

Slightly salted, delicately brittle, unashamedly decadent – the perfect accompaniment to rich desserts.

TO BE EATEN ON ITS OWN OR TO DECORATE 8 DESSERTS

175g golden caster sugar
2 tablespoons golden syrup
4 tablespoons warm water
1 teaspoon Bovril
50g butter
$1/4$ teaspoon smoked paprika
150g toasted flaked almonds

In a heavy-based pan over a medium heat mix together the sugar, golden syrup, warm water and the Bovril. Cook until the mixture is a light golden brown, which should take between 10 and 15 minutes. Remove from the heat and add the butter, paprika and almonds and mix them all together.

Pour the mixture out onto a prepared baking sheet and spread out about $1/2$ cm thick. Leave it to cool completely and then break up into pieces.

ATCHOO!
The power of a good sneeze can exceed 100 miles per hour., The potency of a sneeze can be attributed to the number of organs involved in the process; not just the nose and mouth, but the muscles of the face, throat and chest.

CONSOMMÉ

A much underrated classic clear soup, well worth rediscovering with added Bovril beef richness.

SERVES 6

750g shin of beef, diced
2 tablespoons Bovril dissolved in 300ml boiling water
1.5 litres water
1 medium onion, roughly chopped
1 medium carrot, roughly chopped
1 bay leaf
sea salt and freshly ground black pepper
small wine glass of dry sherry
1 or 2 egg whites with their shells, to clarify (optional)

Put all the ingredients except the seasoning, sherry and the egg whites into a large saucepan. Bring to the boil, removing any scum that forms during cooking. Lower the heat so that the liquid is just at simmering point and cover. Leave to cook for at least an hour.

Strain through a sieve lined with muslin. If not sufficiently clear return to the pan with the unwhisked egg whites and the shells and simmer for a further 10–15 minutes.

Sieve again and return to a clean pan. Add the sherry and season to taste.

This is excellent served with a garnish of freshly cooked vegetables cut into julienne strips and some warm crusty bread.

Opposite
Bovine cuteness
1915

HUMMUS, ROCKET & RED ONION WRAP

You can make this hummus in advance and then create a perfect wrap in no time at all.

MAKES A BATCH OF HUMMUS FOR 8-10

225g chickpeas, soaked overnight in cold water
2 bay leaves
sprig of thyme
1 onion, quartered
2 teaspoons Bovril
6 black peppercorns
3 cloves fresh garlic, peeled and diced
3 tablespoons light tahini (sesame paste)
4 tablespoons olive oil
3 tablespoons freshly squeezed lemon juice
4–5 tablespoons chickpea water
$\frac{1}{2}$ teaspoon ground cumin

For each wrap
1 soft flour tortilla
2 tablespoons hummus
$\frac{1}{4}$ small red onion, finely sliced
small handful fresh rocket or watercress
1 heaped teaspoon natural yoghurt

Drain and rinse the chickpeas, tip into a large saucepan and cover with fresh water. Add the bay leaves, thyme, onion quarters, Bovril and peppercorns and bring to the boil. Boil rapidly for 10 minutes then turn down the heat and simmer for 1 hour until the chickpeas are soft. Drain, reserving at least 5 tablespoons of the chickpea water and allow to cool.

Remove the bay leaves and any stems of thyme and put the chickpeas, onion and peppercorns into a food processor adding the garlic, tahini, half the olive oil, the lemon juice, half the chickpea water and the cumin. Blitz to a coarse purée. Now, with the motor running, add the remaining olive oil and remaining chickpea water until you have the right consistency. You may need to add more chickpea water – you want to end up with a firm, textured consistency. Check and adjust the seasoning to your taste.

For the wraps simply warm the tortillas and spread with the hummus. Top with the red onion and the rocket and finish with a dollop of yoghurt. Roll up the wrap and devour.

10 TON 10 TON

10 TON

Powerful PECULIARS

BEEF AND MUSHROOM STROGANOFF

Cook this wonderful beef and mushroom extravaganza for discerning guests... they'll become friends forever!

SERVES 4-6

500g rump steak, trimmed of any fat
90g unsalted butter
500g button mushrooms, thinly sliced
2 large onions, finely sliced
1 dessertspoon Bovril dissolved in 300ml boiling water
300ml soured cream
nutmeg
sea salt and freshly ground black pepper

Cut the steak into thin strips about $\frac{1}{2}$cm wide and no more than 6cm long.

Melt the butter in a large sauté pan and cook the onions gently until they are very soft but not browned, then remove from the pan and keep to one side. Turn up the heat and add the meat a few pieces at a time and brown. Set aside with the onions.

When all the meat has been browned, reduce the heat, add the mushrooms and cook until starting to soften. You may need to add some extra butter at this point. Return the onion and meat to the pan and pour in the Bovril stock. Bring to the boil and simmer everything together for 10 minutes.

Season and then add the soured cream and a grating of nutmeg. Bring just up to simmering point and then serve with boiled or steamed rice and a green salad.

TON

Strong horny type

The strongest creature on earth? Hmmm... The elephant? Nope, not even close. Whilst our trunked friends can carry loads of up to several tonnes, a proportional evaluation of a very tiny compatriot of Dumbo's reveals strength of an extraordinary kind. Whilst an African elephant can carry about 25 per cent of its own body weight, the rhinoceros beetle can carry an eye-bulging 850 times its own weight (that's the equivalent of Dumbo simultaneously piggy-backing 850 of his brothers and sisters). Such is the rhinoceros beetle's strength that he can forage through the leaves and foliage on jungle floors and burrow underground to safety. Despite their immense power, they live on a modest diet of rotting fruit and sap – not a protein shake in sight!

SAUSAGE JAMBALAYA

This is a really easy and very tasty Deep South American dish, ideally accompanied with a long cool glass of iced bourbon and live jazz.

SERVES 4

2 tablespoons olive oil
2 onions, chopped
2 spring onions, chopped
1 green pepper, deseeded and diced
1 tablespoon chopped fresh parsley
400g tin chopped tomatoes
1 tablespoon tomato ketchup
2 cloves garlic, finely diced
$1/2$ teaspoon dried mint
1 tablespoon Bovril, dissolved in 300ml warm water
300g long grain rice
salt
400g smoked sausage, cut into chunks
$1/4$ teaspoon cayenne pepper

Heat the oil in a deep frying pan and sauté the onions, spring onions, pepper and parsley for 5 minutes.

Add the tomatoes, tomato ketchup, garlic, mint and Bovril stock and bring up to a simmer. Add the rice, a pinch of salt, the sausage and cayenne and then enough water to cover the ingredients by about 3cm.

Cook until at least half of the liquid has been absorbed and then cover and simmer over a very low heat for 45 minutes, resisting the temptation to lift the lid until the end when you will have a delicious red jambalaya.

SILKY STRONG

The spider is one of the world's finest unsung engineers. Their webs are powerful prey-catching tools. The strongest web belongs to the Golden Orb Web Spider, which can be 6 metres tall and 2 metres wide and last for several years.

BOVRIL LAMB KEBABS

Make 'em small for canapés or big for barbecues, these great kebabs are perfect to share with friends.

MAKES 10 BIG KEBABS

1kg lamb neck fillet, cut into 2.5cm chunks
2 teaspoons Bovril
20 small dried apricots
2 red peppers, deseeded and cut into 3cm square
   pieces
20 cherry tomatoes
salt and pepper
chopped fresh mint, to garnish

You will need 10 wooden or metal skewers

Place the diced lamb into a dish and spoon over the Bovril, turning the pieces over until they are all coated. Cover and leave for at least one hour.

When you are ready, lift the lamb from the marinade retaining any juices.

Onto each kebab skewer thread a tomato, then a piece of lamb, then a piece of red pepper, then lamb again, an apricot piece and finally lamb. Prepare 10 skewers. Lay them onto a foil covered grill and pour over any remaining marinade. Season well.

Cook under a hot grill until the lamb is browned outside but still pink inside. Serve on a bed of fluffy rice with a shower of mint.

A beef drink bequeathed

John Lawson Johnston was a dietetic expert. In 1874, three years after the French had lost the Franco-Prussian war, Johnston won a contract to supply one million tins of beef – three years' worth of provisions – to the French government. They believed that poor rations for their soldiers had been a chief factor in the defeat of their country. Johnston moved back to Canada, where he felt he would be better able to meet the supply demand for fulfilling the order. Ten years prior to taking on the contract, Johnston had concocted a recipe for a liquid form of beef. A man not prone to pretension, he gave his recipe the name of 'Johnston's Fluid Beef'. Now back in Canada, he began to experiment further with this broth. He used beef

SAVOURY BREAD AND BUTTER PUDDING

I had this dish cooked for me by one of England's best known TV chefs (no names, no pack-drill!). He wouldn't give me the recipe! I tried my own version, but it was only when I added the Bovril that I had my Eureka! moment.

SERVES 4

2 large slices of slightly stale white bread, crusts removed
butter, for spreading
Bovril, for spreading
90g mature Cheddar cheese, grated
3 large eggs
600ml full-fat milk

Preheat the oven to 150°C/300°F/Gas 2.

Spread the bread with softened butter and then Bovril.

Cut into quarters and arrange half of the bread in an ovenproof dish sprinkling over half the cheese. Repeat.

Beat the eggs with the milk and strain over the bread and cheese.

Leave to stand for at least 10 minutes before baking for $1^1/_4$ hours until just firm. Increase the heat toward the end of cooking time to brown the top or place under a pre-heated grill for a few minutes to crisp.

parts that were left over from the French government's tinned beef order, and began to reinvent the broth as a concentrate. He hit on a winning formula, and trialled selling a hot beef drink at Montreal's freezing-cold winter carnival. A phenomenon was born. Irony struck a few years later, when fire destroyed the business premises that he used to create the very drink that had brought an unprecedented glow to a city that had been so very, very cold. Johnston returned to London and started again, setting up shop in Shoreditch, and beginning to produce and sell the concentrate once more. It could be purchased in pubs and grocery stores. By 1886, a shorter and somewhat more appealing name had been found: Bovril. He formed the word by combining the rather exotic-sounding *Vril* (picked up from a science fiction novel of the day and referring to an 'electric fluid' with restorative powers) and *bos* (the Latin for cow). He registered the name the following year, and just two years later, more than 3,000 bars and public houses up and down the country could be found to serve Johnston's brilliant beef broth.

If you can't beat a bull

join him !

Get the best of a bull with Bovril

Yell for Bovril

Bovril
good and beefy

Bovril
Warms & Cheers

EUROPEAN CHAMPIONSHIP
HENRI DELAUNAY CUP — QUALIFYING T

England
v
Northern
Ireland

WEDNESDAY NOVEMBER 22nd 19
KICK-OFF 7.45 p.m.

WEMBLE

PEANUT & STRAWBERRY RING

This is a great way to show how versatile Bovril really is and what a fantastic taste builder when mixed with peanuts and fruit flavours.

SERVES 4-6

You will need a 20cm ring mould

1 packet strawberry jelly
1 banana, sliced
100g peanuts, chopped
1 teaspoon Bovril
250g crushed pineapple, fresh or tinned
200ml double cream

Make the jelly according to the packet instructions adding the Bovril and then refrigerate. Allow to part set and then fold in the bananas and peanuts. Spoon into a ring mould and continue chilling until firm – about 4 hours.

Dip the ring mould into a bowl of hot water and then turn out onto a large round plate.

Whip the cream into stiff peaks and fold in the pineapple. Fill the centre with the pineapples and cream – really yummy.

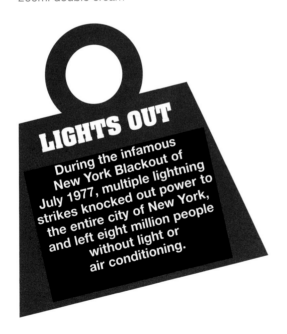

LIGHTS OUT

During the infamous New York Blackout of July 1977, multiple lightning strikes knocked out power to the entire city of New York, and left eight million people without light or air conditioning.

CHILLI BEEF WITH CORNBREAD TOPPING

Not the simplest dish but check out the ingredients and you'll see why it's well worth the effort – it has a real 'wow' factor.

SERVES 4

For the chilli
3–4 tablespoons groundnut or sunflower oil
1 onion, finely chopped
1 red pepper, cut into strips
1 large clove garlic, chopped
500g minced beef
1 teaspoon ground coriander
1 teaspoon ground cumin
2 or 3 small hot red or green chillies, deseeded and
   finely chopped
400g tin chopped tomatoes
2 tablespoons tomato purée
1 dessertspoon Bovril
1 tin red kidney beans, drained and rinsed
freshly ground black pepper

For the cornbread
240g cornmeal
$1/2$ teaspoon fine sea salt
1 tablespoon plain flour
2 teaspoons baking powder
1 large egg
275ml buttermilk
handful of grated Cheddar cheese

Heat the oil in a large saucepan and fry the onion, pepper and garlic. Add the minced beef using a wooden spoon to break up any lumps. Cook until just browned.

Add the coriander, cumin and chillies to the meat mixture then tip in the tomatoes and add the tomato purée, the Bovril and kidney beans. Bring to the boil and simmer for 30–40 minutes adding a little hot water if the mixture looks as if it is drying out too much. You need a moist but not sloppy mixture.

Season with freshly ground black pepper and sea salt (if necessary) then turn into a heatproof dish and heat the oven to 200°C/400°F/Gas 6.

To make the cornbread, mix the dry ingredients in a large bowl then add the egg beaten with the buttermilk.

Pour or drop in spoonfuls over the chilli mixture and sprinkle over some grated Cheddar. Bake for about 30 minutes until golden and bubbling.

FOUR-NUT ROAST

The very words 'nut roast' is likely to send uninspiring shivers down most people's spines, but by combining chestnuts, walnuts, almonds and cashews this nut roast proves to be a very classy dish indeed.

SERVES 4

300g mixed nuts (chestnuts, walnuts, almonds and cashews)
4 shallots, finely diced
400g tin chopped tomatoes
1 free-range egg, beaten
150g Emmental cheese
1 teaspoon dried mixed sage and mint
1 tablespoon chopped fresh flat leaf parsley
2 level teaspoons Bovril mixed with 1 tablespoon boiling water
grated zest of half a lemon
salt and pepper

Preheat the oven to 180°C/350°F/Gas 4.

Place the mixed nuts on a baking tray and put in the oven for 8–10 minutes until golden – taking care not to burn them. Let them cool and then blitz in a processor until ground.

Place the ground nuts in a large bowl add all the other ingredients, finally seasoning with salt and pepper. Mix everything together well.

Line a 1lb loaf tin with baking parchment and spoon in the nutty mixture and bake for 1 hour until firm to the touch and golden.

Leave to cool for 10 minutes and then turn out the nut loaf. Delicious with cranberry sauce and fresh peppery watercress.

Bless thy Bovril

Not many storecupboard stocks and spreads come with Papal approval, but an audacious advert from the end of the nineteenth century depicts the Pope seated on throne and gripping a steaming mug of hot Bovril in one hand and blessing our beloved beef extract with the other! The advert was emblazoned with, 'The Two Infallible Powers – The Pope & Bovril'! And Bovril has remained infallible: worshipping of its meaty goodness has continued unabated for a hundred years and more! (See illustration over page.)

THE TWO INFALLIBLE POWERS.
THE POPE & BOVRIL.

PORK CHOPS WITH BRANDIED TOMATO GRAVY

This is fast food at its best for a perfectly relaxed evening meal.

SERVES 2

vegetable oil, for frying
2 pork chops
25g butter
1 tablespoon plain flour
small tin of chopped tomatoes
1 tin consommé
1 tablespoon brandy
1 teaspoon Bovril
chopped parsley, to garnish

Preheat the oven to 180°C/350°F/Gas 4.

Heat the oil in a frying pan and brown the chops for 2–3 minutes on each side. Transfer the chops to the oven and cook for 8 minutes.

Melt the butter in a pan and then add the flour. Cook for 1 minute, stirring constantly. Add the remaining ingredients, bring up to the boil and then simmer for 5 minutes until the sauce has thickened.

Remove the chops from the oven and onto warm plates. Pour over the rich gravy and serve scattered with parsley.

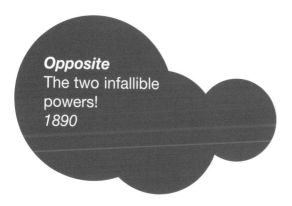

Opposite
The two infallible powers!
1890

CHINESE-STYLE PORK WITH BOVRIL SAUCE

There's a reason we've all loved Bovril for so long: its wonderful meaty flavour brings fusion to dishes from all around the world. This is a fine example.

SERVES 4

2 teaspoons light soy sauce
500g pork shoulder, cubed
2 tablespoons groundnut or sunflower oil
2 teaspoons freshly grated ginger
3 cloves garlic, finely grated
1 medium onion, finely sliced
1 red pepper, deseeded and finely sliced
1 rounded teaspoon Bovril dissolved in 300ml boiling water
2 teaspoons cornflour

Sprinkle the soy sauce over the pork pieces in a shallow dish and leave to marinate for half an hour.

Heat the oil in a wok and fry the pork until cooked through, then set aside.

Next, fry the ginger, garlic, onion and pepper. Cook until the vegetables are just tender.

Return the pork to the pan then pour over the Bovril stock. Bring to the boil and simmer for 3–4 minutes so that the meat is thoroughly hot.

Mix the cornflour with three tablespoons of water in a small basin and add to the wok. Stir the contents of the pan until the sauce has thickened. Serve with steamed rice.

Other vegetables can be added like broccoli, spinach, pak choi, bean sprouts and green beans and you can also substitute the pork shoulder for thin slices of rump steak or chicken.

POTENT PONG

The dubious honour of the world's smelliest cheese went to a French effort called Vieux Boulogne, made from cow's milk by cheesemaker Philippe Olivier, and judged by an olfactory panel at Cranfield University in 2004.

PROMOTES THAT SINGING FEELING
-The "accompaniment" of perfect health

Opposite
Bovril's pyjama-clad advocate of the 1930s

BOVRIL NOODLE SOUP

This is a new take on a dish which has been served for as long as Bovril has been around. Check out the flavour fusions of ginger, garlic, star anise and coriander.

SERVES 2

1 dessertspoon Bovril dissolved in 600ml boiling water
6 slices of fresh ginger the thickness of a pound coin
1 clove garlic, thinly sliced
2 star anise
1 tablespoon nam pla (fish sauce)
freshly ground black pepper
60g egg or rice noodles
120g rump or rib-eye steak, cut into very thin strips
fresh coriander
4 finely sliced spring onions
small handful of beansprouts

Simmer the Bovril stock with the ginger, garlic and star anise for 30 minutes, topping up with extra boiling water as necessary. Strain the liquid, discarding the spices, and garlic and then stir in the nam pla.

Add the noodles to the stock and simmer for a few minutes until just cooked.

Ladle the noodles and stock into warm bowls into which you have placed the strips of meat, which will cook in the heat from the liquid.

Scatter over a little freshly chopped coriander, the spring onions and some beansprouts.

H-H-H-HOT

The world's hottest chilli is the Bhut Jolokia. That translates as 'ghost chilli' and is from the northeastern region of India. Chilli strength is measured by the content of capsaicin within. It is the capsaicin that generates the sensation of heat.

RABBIT STEW

You don't have to flame this stew but it does create a great spectacle at the table and well worth the effort.

SERVES 4

1 rabbit (approx. 1.5kg)
2 tablespoons seasoned flour
2 tablespoons vegetable oil
200g unsmoked streaky bacon, diced
2 onions, roughly chopped
2 sticks of celery, diced
400g chestnut mushrooms, sliced
1 tablespoon Bovril mixed with 200ml boiling water
300ml dry white wine
few sprigs fresh thyme
2 bay leaves
salt and black pepper
2 slices white bread, crusts removed
1 tablespoon Dijon mustard
2 tablespoons brandy
4 tablespoons sour cream

Preheat the oven to 160°C/325°F/Gas 3.

Cut the rabbit up into portions and put into a large bowl. Dust with the seasoned flour and turn the pieces to coat all over. Then shake them in a sieve or colander to release the excess flour.

Heat the oil in a large flameproof casserole, add the bacon and onion and cook for a few minutes to release the bacon juices. Add the rabbit pieces and gently brown all over. When this is done add the celery, mushrooms, Bovril stock, wine and herbs and season with salt and pepper.

Spread the bread slices with the mustard and arrange them over the top of the casserole, mustard side down. Put on the lid and pop it into the oven to cook for 1–1$\frac{1}{2}$ hours or until the meat is tender.

Remove the casserole from the oven and stir to disperse the bread throughout the juices. Cook, covered, for a further 30 minutes.

Take out the casserole and add the sour cream then leave aside to rest for 10 minutes. When you are ready to serve heat the brandy in a small pan, place the casserole in the centre of the table, flame the brandy and pour it over the rabbit stew – wow!

SPAGHETTI ALLA CARRETTIERA

Originally the cart-driver's pasta – now anyone can enjoy it!

SERVES 4

2 tablespoons olive oil
50g pancetta, diced
1 clove garlic, finely diced
300g mixed wild mushrooms, wiped and roughly sliced
1 level teaspoon Bovril
100ml vermouth (or white wine)
300g dried spaghetti
50g canned tuna, flaked
chopped fresh parsley
freshly grated Parmesan, to serve
salt and black pepper

Heat the olive oil in a large frying pan and gently sauté the pancetta and garlic until the fat on the pancetta has become translucent. Add the mushrooms, Bovril, season with plenty of black pepper, then pour in the vermouth. Cook for 5 minutes.

Heat a large pan of salted water. When boiling, add the pasta and cook for 8–10 minutes until just al dente.

Add the tuna to the mushrooms and bacon, gently mixing it with the other sauce ingredients without breaking it up too much and then scatter the parsley all over. Take off the heat and cover to keep warm while you drain the pasta.

Serve the spaghetti in warm bowls with the sauce spooned over and serve with a bowl of freshly grated Parmesan cheese. The Italians do not traditionally eat Parmesan with fish but it does lend itself rather well to this dish.

The Beautiful Game

Bovril has a long association with football. Traditionally, the winter terraces would be packed with thermos-clutching fanatics, cheering on their team whilst drinking down their warming cup of beef tea. In the 1960s, Chelsea and England striker Jimmy Greaves became the face of Bovril, proclaiming he 'wouldn't be without it'. The first link between football and Bovril was in 1898, when the FA-Cup winning team of that year, Nottingham Forest, put their name (and attributed part of their success!) to the nutritional qualities of the drink. The drink was and still is immensely popular across Scottish football grounds (after all, its inventor was a Scot!).

BOVRIL and a clever Cook.

(One of the prize-winners in the Bovril Competition)

STEAK & KIDNEY PUDDING

We don't make puddings any more – more's the pity! Let's hope this Bovril-enhanced classic dish will help reinstate a glorious British tradition.

SERVES 4

450g diced chuck steak
150g ox kidney, cores removed and diced
1 onion, finely chopped
salt and freshly ground black pepper
1 teaspoon fresh thyme leaves
$^1/_4$ teaspoon mustard powder
1 tablespoon plain flour
1 tablespoon Bovril dissolved in 150ml warm water

For the suet pastry
225g self-raising flour
salt and freshly ground black pepper
100g shredded beef suet
6–8 tablespoons cold water

You will need a $1^1/_2$ pint lightly greased pudding basin

Opposite
A key component
in a cook's craft!
c. end of 19th Century

Put the steak and kidney in a bowl together with the onion, thyme and mustard powder then season with salt and plenty of black pepper. Turn the meat to mix well and set aside.

Sift the flour into a large bowl and season with a good pinch of salt and some black pepper. Add the suet and mix well, then gradually add enough of the water to create a soft, elastic dough.

Turn the dough out onto a lightly floured board and cut off about a quarter of it for the lid. Roll out the remaining dough sufficient to line the pudding basin with about a 1cm overhang.

Next, add the flour to the meat mixture and ensure it is coated well. Put it all in a sieve and shake off any excess flour. Add the meat to the pudding basin without pushing it down and then pour in the Bovril stock – enough to fill two-thirds of the way up the meat.

Roll out the remaining suet pastry to create a lid over the meat and then fold the border over and press the pastry together to seal. Cover the bowl with a double layer of foil with a pleat in the middle to allow for expansion and tie this in place with some string. Steam the pudding for 4 hours, topping up with boiling water as required.

To serve, turn out onto a warm plate and cut out wedges of steaming pud.

BOVRIL AND MOLASSES PECAN PIE

The wonderful thing about Bovril is that you can substitute it for salt in a recipe and get a much bigger and fuller flavour from the dish. This is a classic example of Bovril at its most versatile.

SERVES 6

500g pack short crust pastry
170g light brown sugar
170g molasses
20g melted butter
4 eggs, lightly beaten
1 teaspoon Bovril
1 teaspoon vanilla essence
325g chopped pecans

WED LOCK!

In 2006, the male and female holders of the respective Arm Wrestling Champion of the World titles were Californian husband-and-wife team Allen and Carolyn Fisher. They have been holding hands for over twenty years!

The pastry must be defrosted completely if you buy frozen.

Pre-heat the oven to 200°C/400°F/Gas 6.

Roll out the pastry on a lightly floured surface to about the thickness of a £1 coin and line a 20cm ovenproof flan dish with the pastry, trimming the edges. Put it in the refrigerator for 10 minutes.

In the meantime, in a heavy based pan over a medium heat blend the brown sugar, molasses, butter, eggs, Bovril and vanilla. Cook for a few minutes until all the ingredients are mixed well together then stir in the pecans.

Take the pastry-lined dish from the refrigerator and pour in the pecan mixture. Cook for 10 minutes and then reduce the temperature to 180°C/350°F/Gas 4 for a further 10 minutes or until the pie has set.

Take it out of the oven and let it cool before serving topped with fresh seasonal fruit.

LEMON & THYME ROAST CHICKEN

If you ever thought chicken lacked taste then try this way of cooking in delicious flavour leaving the bird succulent whether eaten hot or cold.

SERVES 4-6

1 free-range chicken (about 1.5kg)
2 teaspoons Bovril
1 lemon
freshly ground black pepper
8 rashers smoked streaky bacon
3 cloves garlic, peeled and halved
3 shallots, peeled and halved
2 sprigs fresh thyme

Preheat the oven to 180°C/350°F/Gas 4.

Place the chicken in a roasting pan and spread the whole bird with a thin layer of Bovril. Cut the lemon in half and squeeze the juice over the Bovril. Now cover the bird with lashings of freshly milled black pepper and finally lay the rashers of smoked bacon over all of it. Fill the inside of the chicken with the garlic, shallots and thyme and the remainder of the lemon.

When the oven is up to temperature pop the chicken in and cook for 1½ hours, removing the bacon after 1 hour but keeping it beside the chicken in the pan.

Serve with crispy pan-fried cabbage and baby roast potatoes.

Staggering Stories of STRENGTH

LENTIL DHAL WITH GINGER AND CORIANDER

One of the many wonderful things about cooking lentil dhal is the great spicy, appetite-promoting aroma as the dish develops in the pan.

SERVES 4-6

2 tablespoons vegetable oil (or to be totally authentic 60g ghee)
1 medium onion, diced
1 clove garlic, peeled and diced
1 fresh chilli, finely diced
2cm fresh ginger, finely diced
2 tomatoes, skinned and roughly chopped
1 teaspoon turmeric
1 teaspoon cumin seeds
2 teaspoons Bovril
hot water
250g red lentils, washed and drained
2 tablespoons fresh chopped coriander

Heat the oil (or ghee) in a large pan over a medium heat. Add the onion, garlic, chilli and ginger and fry until the onion just begins to colour. Then add the tomatoes, turmeric, cumin, Bovril and a couple of tablespoons of water then add the lentils and turn up the heat to give a rolling boil.

Cook for 5 minutes and then turn the heat to low and let it simmer for 15–20 minutes adding a little more hot water to achieve the right consistency. When it's ready, stir in the fresh coriander and serve.

Thick-necked

Englishman John Evans is a professional 'head balancer'. At more than two metres tall and over twenty-four stone in weight, he's not a man of insignificant size. But the vital statistic is his 24-inch neck. It has enabled him to steady books, bricks and beer barrels using just his anatomical attic for support. He has also balanced people and has branched out into speedboats, quad bikes and automobiles.

His most well-known challenge was balancing a Mini weighing 162kg on his head. A mere sniff of wind can spell disaster for this Derbyshire-born master of stability, since it's only his neck that keeps such huge weights safely propped up. A sway, trip or tumble could cripple him as the loads that he dares to balance are more extreme than any below-neck musculature could possibly cope with. Evans is the holder of 32 World Records and has raised thousands and thousands of pounds for charitable causes.

CHEESE AND ONION FRITTATA

Eaten hot or cold this Bovril infused classic frittata packs some great taste.

SERVES 2-3

4 eggs
50g single cream
freshly ground black pepper
pinch of chilli powder
2 tablespoons Bovril
1 tablespoon butter
1 tablespoon olive oil
2 medium onions, peeled and roughly chopped
2 medium potatoes, peeled and thinly sliced
50g grated strong mature Cheddar cheese
1 heaped teaspoon chopped parsley

Pre-heat the grill to medium hot.

In a mixing bowl whisk the eggs, cream, pepper, chilli powder and Bovril. This needs to be light and frothy.

Put the butter and oil into a large frying pan over a medium heat and add the onions and potatoes and fry for 10–12 minutes until they begin to colour.

Pour the egg mixture over the onions and potatoes and cook for 3–4 minutes over a low heat then sprinkle the cheese and parsley over the top. Cook for a further couple of minutes and then put the pan under the grill for another 2 minutes until the cheese melts and just starts to bubble.

Cut into wedges and serve with dressed mixed leaves.

Opposite
Bovine invigoration!
1915

BOVRIL

Bovril soon puts a man on his feet

ROASTED RED PEPPER RISOTTO

It seems that risotto is becoming one of the nation's favourite dishes. When you've cooked this recipe with its deep seated flavours you'll see why.

SERVES 2-3

2 large red peppers
2 tablespoons olive oil
1 teaspoon Bovril
600ml chicken stock
$\frac{1}{2}$ teaspoon ground cumin
$\frac{1}{2}$ teaspoon ground coriander
$\frac{1}{4}$ teaspoon chilli powder
2 leeks, white parts only, finely sliced
1 clove garlic
200g Arborio rice
1 tablespoon butter
2 tablespoons grated Parmesan cheese

Preheat the oven to 180°C/350°F/Gas 4.

Halve and deseed the peppers, discarding any pith. Heat 1 tablespoon of the olive oil and stir in the Bovril. Use this to brush the peppers all over and then put them in a baking tin in the oven for 15–20 minutes until just beginning to soften and char. Remove the peppers, allow to cool a little, cut into chunks and leave aside.

In a small pan bring the chicken stock to a simmer then add the cumin, coriander and chilli.

While this is simmering, heat the remaining oil and the butter in a heavy based frying pan and, when sizzling, add the leeks and sauté for 5 minutes. Then add the garlic and rice and cook for 1 minute, stirring all the time. Next add half the stock and all of the peppers, turn the heat down to medium, and keep stirring.

Once the liquid is almost absorbed, still stirring occasionally, gradually add more stock, a little at a time, until the rice is tender and creamy but not dry (you may not need all of the stock). Remove the pan from the heat, stir in the cheese and serve at once.

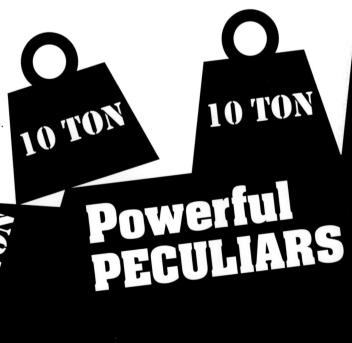

AMERICAN MEATLOAF

Serve this fantastic meatloaf hot with a tomato sauce and seasonal vegetables or cold with pickles and salad.

SERVES 4-6

30g unsalted butter
1 medium onion, finely chopped
750g minced beef
1 dessertspoon Bovril
1 large free-range egg
120g fresh white breadcrumbs
2 tablespoons chopped parsley
1 tablespoon thyme leaves
sea salt and freshly ground black pepper

Pre heat the oven to 180°C/350°F/Gas 4.

Melt the butter in a small pan and cook the onion until soft, but not browned.

Combine all the remaining ingredients in a large bowl, add the onion, mixing well, and turn into a greased loaf tin.

Bake for about $1^1/_2$ hours basting occasionally with stock made from dissolving 1 further teaspoon of Bovril in 150ml boiling water.

Allow to cool a little before turning out to serve.

TON

Strong to the finish

Does spinach make you strong? Well, we have a cartoon character and a data entry error to thank for perpetuating one of the most commonly believed myths in food. Popeye was the heroic, spinach-guzzling Sailorman whose redoubtable physical strength was put down to the gallons of canned green leaves he consumed. But it was some sixty years prior to Popeye's first comic-strip outing, way back in 1870, that one man's mistake was accepted for fact. A German scientist, Dr E. von Wolf, was conducting a study into the iron content of the vegetable. In recording his findings, von Wolf contrived to misplace a decimal point and thus inflated the strength-giving properties of spinach to ten times its actual value! Broccoli and cauliflower actually have a higher iron content.

MOROCCAN STUFFED LEG OF LAMB

A dish 'stuffed' full of Moroccan sunshine.

SERVES 6-8

60g pine nuts
150g cous cous
250ml boiling water
1 vegetable stock cube
100g frozen petit pois
6 ready to eat dried prunes, stoned and roughly
   chopped
small handful fresh mint, chopped
salt and pepper
boned leg of lamb
2 tablespoons Bovril

FATAL FROG
The dart poison frog of Central and Southern America produces the most powerful venom of any animal. Secreted in glands on their skin, just two tenths of a microgram is lethal for humans. Beware fair maidens in search of a prince!

Preheat the oven to 180°C/350°F/Gas 4.

Spread the pine nuts on a baking sheet and toast them in the oven for 5 minutes until golden. Remove and leave to cool.

Put the cous cous into a bowl. Combine the boiling water and stock cube, stir well then pour it over the cous cous. Leave for 5 minutes and then fluff it up with a fork. Add the peas, prunes, mint and pine nuts, season well and combine all the ingredients.

Spread the lamb out flat on a board and spread half of the Bovril all over the inside of the lamb. Pile the stuffing down the centre of the leg of lamb and then bring up the meat from the sides. Tie securely into a roll. (Any unused stuffing can be rolled into golf-sized balls and added to the roasting tin for the last half-hour of cooking.)

Put the lamb into a roasting tin and cook for $1-1\frac{1}{2}$ hours, depending on how you like your lamb cooked. Halfway through the cooking time remove the lamb from the oven, spoon out a couple of tablespoons of the juices and mix with the remaining Bovril. Baste the lamb with these meaty juices and continue cooking.

When the lamb is cooked to your liking, remove it from the oven and leave to stand in a warm dish for 10 minutes to relax the meat before serving in thick, juicy slices.

OATCAKES

Try these as the perfect vehicle for breakfast, loaded with bacon, scrambled eggs, smoked salmon or your favourite preserve.

MAKES 16 OATCAKES

115g medium oatmeal
1 teaspoon sea salt
115g plain flour
55g lard or butter
1 rounded dessertspoon Bovril

For the egg wash
1 egg beaten with a little milk

Preheat the oven to 180°C/350°F/Gas 4.

Mix the oatmeal, salt and flour together in a bowl and rub in the fat as if making pastry. Dissolve the Bovril in three tablespoons of hot water. Add to the other ingredients and mix well. You may need to add a little extra water to give a soft but not sticky dough.

Roll the dough out thinly and cut into rounds using a 3"/7.5cm plain cutter. Arrange the rounds on baking sheets lined with parchment and brush with the egg glaze.

Bake in the centre of the oven for 10 minutes. Remove from the oven and egg wash again. Return to the oven and cook for a further 10 minutes or until firm and nicely browned.

Store in an airtight container when cool.

Opposite
Chopper to the rescue!
1958

SWEET AND SOUR POT ROAST

Delicious long slow-cooked beef exuding intense tongue-tingling flavours.

SERVES 6-8

2kg rolled rib of beef
150g smoked streaky bacon
30g lard
1 tablespoon sunflower oil
1 large onion, finely chopped
2 cloves garlic, diced
4 tablespoons Bovril
250ml red wine vinegar
1 teaspoon mixed dried herbs
1 tablespoon mango chutney
1 tablespoon finely diced stem ginger
50g pitted green olives
6 baby shallots

Heat the oven to 220°C/425°F/Gas 7.

Lay the rib of beef out flat and cover with strips of bacon, roll up and tie and place in a roasting dish with the lard and pop in the oven to brown for 15 minutes.

Meanwhile, in a frying pan heat the cooking oil and sauté the onions and garlic until soft, then add the Bovril, wine vinegar, herbs and mango chutney and mix them well together.

Remove the meat pan from the oven and turn it down to 150°C/300°F/Gas 2. Tip the contents of the frying pan over the meat, cover with kitchen foil and pop it back in the oven for 1 hour (if you like your beef well done increase this time to $1\frac{1}{2}$ hours).

Remove the meat from the oven, add the stem ginger, the olives and the shallots to the roasting pan and cook for a further 20 minutes, still covered.

When the rib of beef is cooked let it stand for 10 minutes, keeping it warm and then serve in thick slices spooning over the thick sauce.

TURKEY BANG BANG

A great way of using up leftover cooked chicken or turkey. The 'bang bang' comes from the chilli sauce.

SERVES 4-6

For the sauce
2 teaspoons sunflower oil
3 tablespoons peanut butter
2 tablespoons chilli sauce
1 dessertspoon Bovril
1 tablespoon caster sugar
1 tablespoon white wine vinegar
3 tablespoons water

For the meat and salad
1 iceberg lettuce, finely shredded
half a cucumber, in slices or batons
small bunch of fresh coriander
small bunch of mint
300g cold turkey
bunch of spring onions, finely sliced
half a red pepper, deseeded and finely sliced

To make the sauce simply combine all the ingredients in a small bowl.

Next, arrange the shredded lettuce on a large platter, followed by the cucumber, then scatter over the roughly chopped coriander and mint. Drizzle over some of the sauce.

Combine the rest of the sauce with the cold meat cut or torn into even sized pieces and arrange this over the lettuce bed.

To finish, scatter over the finely chopped spring onions and the red pepper which has been very thinly sliced.

Boldly go with Bovril...

From the earliest advertising, Bovril has been promoted as a healthy hot drink. In those very early years, testimonials rained in from such eminent figures as the Antarctic explorers Robert Falcon Scott and Ernest Shackleton. Abandoned South-Pole supply huts remain where stores of all manner of tinned goods were found, Bovril among them, Indeed, it was Shackleton who would coin the phrase that would become the very lynchpin for a future renowned Bovril advertising campaign: 'It must be Bovril'. The campaign became particularly pertinent during the First World War, when Bovril was being promoted to help ward off 'flu and chills'.

BOVRIL CHIPS

This is so easy to do and everyone loves these Bovril-flavoured crispy chips. Perfect with most fish dishes especially home-made fish fingers!

SERVES 4

750g Maris Piper, King Edwards or Sante potatoes
4 tablespoons sunflower oil
2 tablespoons Bovril
$\frac{1}{2}$ teaspoon paprika

Preheat the oven to 180°C/350°F/Gas 4

Peel the potatoes and cut them into chunky chips. Rinse in cold water to remove the starch, boil them in unsalted water for 5 minutes remove and drain. Return them to the pan and give the pan a shake to fluff up their edges.

Meanwhile heat the oil with the paprika and Bovril in a roasting tray in a hot oven for 5 minutes. Take the roasting tray out of the oven, stir the Bovril oil well and carefully slide in the chips using a slotted spoon to roll them in the pan juices, making sure they are all completely coated. Return the tray to the oven for 10–12 minutes then take it out again and pour off the fat. Put it back in for 5 minutes or until the Bovril chips are golden and crispy.

JAW ACHE

Many muscles could stake a claim for strongest muscle in the body – the always-at-work eyeballs and heart to name but two – but if strength is defined as the ability to exert a force on an external object then it is the masseter (jaw muscle) with its quite awesome bite strength that would be the outright winner.

BOVRIL
puts a smile into Vegetables

TAKE A TEASPOONFUL OF BOVRIL AND ST

BOVR

MANUFACTURED
BOVRIL LTD & CO
ENGLAND

... rich, satisfying goodness in your vegetable dishes, make ... rule to make them with Bovril. Bovril adds enjoyment ... helps you to assimilate your other food. Always keep Bovril in the kitchen—ask for it at your grocer's.

(Obtainable in 1 oz., 2 oz., 4 oz. and 8 oz. Bottles).

Reflective glory
*Oppsite from 1925
and this page from the
late 1930s*

PUFF PASTRY TWISTS

Cheese straws are out, Bovril-infused puff pastry twists are in!

MAKES 20-24 PUFF PASTRY TWISTS

500g readymade puff pastry
Bovril, for spreading
1 egg beaten with 3 tablespoons full-fat milk
1–2 tablespoons poppy seeds

Pre-heat the oven to 220°C/425°F/Gas 7. Line two large baking sheets or trays with baking parchment.

Roll out the pastry thinly to something less than the thickness of a pound coin. Spread thinly with Bovril then cut into strips 15cm by 1cm.

Twist the pastry strips into spirals and lay carefully on the baking sheets. Brush with the egg glaze and sprinkle generously with poppy seeds.

Bake for 15–20 minutes until risen, golden and crispy.

Billboard Bovril

Bovril became neon-lit in 1909, when its first electrical advertising sign was erected in London's Piccadilly Circus. The first illuminated signs appeared here in 1893, and Bovril was one of the earliest advertisers, hanging around for many years, as part of what would become the oldest and best-known lights complex in the world. But even when their messages were not illuminated, they were potent. There have been many memorable campaigns over Bovril's long life, with popular characters and advertising slogans that still resonate brightly today. 'Liquid life', 'Bovril, one of the pleasures of life' and 'Yell for Bovril' worked and retain a magic both then and now.

BEEF & ONION FLATBREADS

These flatbreads make the perfect party food to serve with spicy dips.

SERVES 4

For the bread base
250g strong plain white flour
$^1/_2$ teaspoon fine sea salt
1 teaspoon active yeast
1 tablespoon olive oil
approx. 125ml warm water

Meat mixture
250g minced beef
1 large clove garlic, finely chopped
1 medium onion, finely chopped
1 teaspoon ground cumin
squeeze of lemon juice or a tablespoon pomegranate
    molasses (if available)
2 tablespoons coarsely chopped flat leaf parsley
sea salt and black pepper
Bovril for spreading
400g tin chopped tomatoes, drained of excess liquid

To make the bread dough mix the flour, salt and yeast together in a large bowl. Dribble in the olive oil and enough warm water to make a soft but not sticky dough. Knead briefly then cover and leave to rise until doubled in size.

While the dough is rising, turn the beef, the garlic and the finely chopped onion into a saucepan and cook gently until the meat loses its pinkness breaking up any lumps with a wooden spoon or fork. Add the ground cumin, the lemon juice or pomegranate molasses and season with salt and black pepper. When the mixture has cooled add the chopped parsley.

Knock back the dough and turn out onto a floured work surface and knead for a couple of minutes until you have springy dough.

Divide into four and roll and stretch each piece into a thin, roughly circular shape. Do this directly onto an oiled baking sheet. You will probably need two sheets.

Spread each of the pieces of dough with Bovril and a quarter of the drained tomato and top with a quarter of the meat mixture.

Leave to prove while you heat the oven to 220°C/425°F/Gas mark 7. When the oven is hot, slide in the trays and bake for 10–15 minutes until the dough is cooked and just starting to take colour. As soon as the breads come out of the oven cover with a clean tea towel and leave for five minutes. This traps the steam and keeps the bread malleable. You should be able to fold the breads so that they can be eaten with your fingers.

Scatter with more chopped parsley before serving with a crunchy salad.

HAND-RAISED PORK PIE

**So many people say they have never had a really
good pork pie – this will change their opinion.**

You will need a 6"/15cm pork pie tin or similar cake tin

For the filling
675g pork shoulder (because you need a bit of fat),
   coarsely chopped
100g unsmoked back bacon, coarsely chopped
$1/_2$ teaspoon dried sage
$1/_2$ teaspoon dried thyme
$1/_4$ teaspoon anchovy essence
$1/_4$ teaspoon ground nutmeg
lots of freshly ground black pepper

For the hot water pastry
340g plain flour
$1/_4$ teaspoon ground mace
150ml water
140g lard
2 teaspoons Bovril
1 free-range egg, beaten

For the jellied stock
250ml vegetable stock
$1/_2$ onion - finely diced
1 bay leaf
4 black peppercorns
$1/_2$ teaspoon dried thyme
1 leaf of gelatine – prepare as per the packet
   instructions

Preheat the oven to 170°C/325°F/Gas 3.

Chop the pork and bacon and put them into a mixing
bowl, add all the other filling ingredients and combine
them all well. Set aside.

Now, to make the pastry. Sieve the flour into a dry bowl
and add the lard and Bovril, stir well, and when all is
dissolved pour it into the dry ingredients immediately.
Stir to form a dough, turn the dough out onto a working
surface and knead lightly and quickly for 5 minutes, but
no more – it is important to work with the pastry while
it's still warm. Take $3/_4$ of the dough, make it into a ball, and
place it in the bottom of your tin. With your fingers work
the dough up the sides of the tin just leaving enough
overlap at the top to fold over later. The $1/_4$ of dough
left is for the round lid and decoration.

Pack the the meat mixture firmly into the pastry case,
right up to the top, and fold over the surplus pastry.
Cut a lid and pop it on the top pinching the pastry
together to seal. Make a 'steam' hole in the top and
brush the pie with beaten egg. Cook for about 2 hours.
Keep an eye on it as ovens do vary. It should come out
golden brown. Place on a cooling tray and leave to cool.

Now for the lush jelly. Pour the vegetable stock into a
pan adding the onion, bay leaf, peppercorns and thyme.
Bring to the boil and simmer until reduced to about
half. Strain into another pan and add the gelatine, stir,
allow to cool a little until syrupy, and then carefully
pour into the cold cooked pork pie via the steam hole.
When the pie is full, chill in the fridge to set the jelly.

PEANUT BOVRIL CRUNCHIES

The kids will love these – pop them in the lunch box and they'll be the envy of their mates!

MAKES 16-20

butter, for greasing
350g self-raising flour
2 teaspoons baking powder
50g unsalted peanuts, crushed
2 teaspoons Bovril dissolved in 200ml warm water
150g crunchy peanut butter
milk for brushing

Preheat the oven to 180°C/350°F/Gas 4.
Grease a baking sheet with a little butter.

Mix together the sieved flour, baking powder and half the peanuts in a bowl. Add the warm Bovril and the peanut butter and stir everything together really well until you have a slightly marbled mixture.

Spread this out on the baking sheet with a palette knife to a depth of 1.5 cm, brush with a little milk and sprinkle over the remaining peanuts.

Bake in the centre of the oven for 45 minutes then turn out and cool on a wire rack. Break into chunks and share them about.

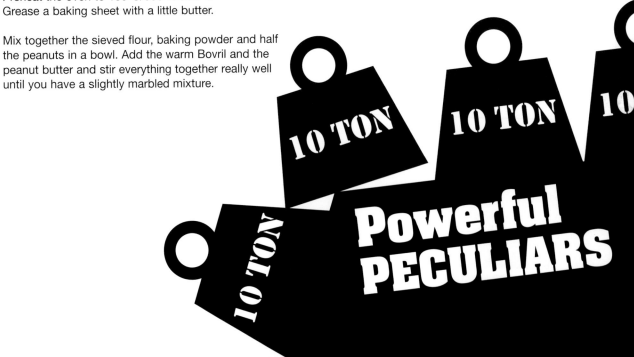

10 TON   10 TON   10

10 TON

Powerful
PECULIARS

BOVRIL & PAPRIKA BELLY PORK

Serve this crispy pork in thick slices drizzled with the sauce and a crispy salad on the side.

SERVES 6

1.5kg belly pork in one piece, skin on
1 teaspoon salt
1 tablespoon smoked paprika

For the sauce
3 tablespoons olive oil
2 cloves garlic, chopped
1 teaspoon fresh ginger, grated
1 small red chilli
3 spring onions, chopped
1 teaspoon smoked paprika
1 teaspoon Bovril
1 tablespoon sweet sherry
handful fresh coriander

Preheat the oven to 180°C/350°F/Gas 4.

Place the piece of pork on a rack over a baking tin, score it with a sharp knife and pour half a kettle of boiling water over it. Pat it dry with kitchen paper and discard the water. This will help the skin to crisp. Sprinkle the salt and paprika over the skin and rub it in well amongst the slits. Put the pork in the centre of the hot oven, still on its rack over the roasting tin, and cook for 2 hours.

To make the sauce, heat the olive oil and add the garlic, ginger, chilli and spring onions and sauté until just golden. Remove from the heat and tip into a food processor. Add the paprika, Bovril, sherry and coriander and blitz to a smooth sauce.

Mental toughness

In 2008, still basking in the success of its hosting of the Olympic Games, Beijing hosted the first ever World Mind Sports Games. Just shy of 3,000 competitors challenged for 35 gold medals across five different board and card game events – chess, bridge, draughts, Go and Chinese chess: representative of some of the oldest and most sophisticated mental exercises known to man. Delegations from each participating country were asked to bring water from their home country to symbolise the source of human spirit. The waters were mixed together and at the end of the games, each delegation returned home with a sample that represented the combined wisdoms of the world. The Games was the brainchild of Frenchman José Damiani, whose wish it was to stage a mental version of the Games in the same Olympic city that held the physical Games.

LAMB & LEEK CASSEROLE

In today's hustle-bustle world its very easy to go for the quick dinner option. Make this the day before and experience a casserole that will make your taste buds roll!

SERVES 4

2 tablespoons sunflower oil
1 onion, roughly chopped
800g diced lamb
450g leeks, diced
1 clove garlic, finely diced
1 teaspoon dried mixed herbs
2 tablespoons Bovril mixed with 250ml warm water
150ml white wine
500g waxy potatoes, peeled and thinly sliced
salt and black pepper
few sprigs of rosemary to garnish

Preheat the oven to 160°C/325°F/Gas 3.

Heat the oil in a flameproof casserole on top of the stove and gently fry the onions until translucent. Add the lamb, moving it around the casserole to brown it all over until the juices flow and then add the leeks, garlic and herbs. Cover and cook over a low heat for 10 minutes.

Remove the casserole from the heat and season the lamb with a pinch of salt and plenty of black pepper. Now layer the potatoes all over the top of the lamb mixture and then pour the Bovril stock and wine over the top. Season with a little more salt and pepper. Cover and cook in the oven for 2 hours.

Remove the casserole from the oven, dot a few pieces of butter over the potatoes and return the casserole to the oven for a further 20 minutes to brown and crisp the potato topping. Serve with sprigs of rosemary.

Opposite
Casserole delayed...
1937

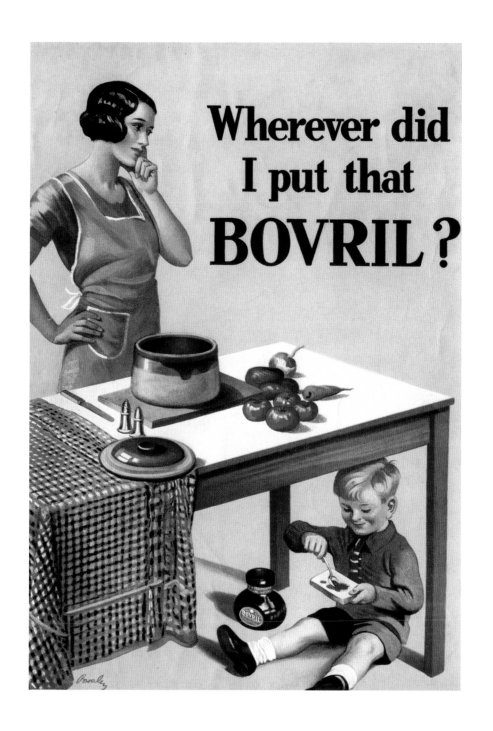

JEWELLED SALAD WITH BOVRIL VINAIGRETTE

This is a sumptuous robust summer salad with a fully structured vinaigrette.

SERVES 4 AS A SIDE DISH

For the Bovril vinaigrette
5 dessertspoons white wine vinegar
1 teaspoon whole grain mustard
freshly ground black pepper
2 teaspoons Bovril
9 dessertspoons good olive oil

10 Romaine or Cos lettuce leaves
4 fresh, firm plum tomatoes roughly chopped
1 large red onion, roughly chopped
1 green pepper, deseeded and cut into rough chunks
1 yellow pepper, deseeded and cut into rough chunks
$\frac{1}{2}$ cucumber cut into 2cm pieces
12 pimento stuffed green olives
finely chopped mint leaves

In a blender put the vinegar, mustard, generous grinds of black pepper and the Bovril and give it a whiz, with the motor still running drizzle in the olive oil and you will have thick vinaigrette. Pour into a jug or bowl and set aside.

Take a salad bowl and line the outside with the lettuce leaves standing them up like soldiers. Mix together the tomatoes, onion, peppers, cucumber and olives and pile them into the centre. Using a dessertspoon or ladle generously drizzle the vinaigrette over the salad and finish with a flourish of mint.

The remaining vinaigrette can be stored in an airtight container in the fridge for up to a week.

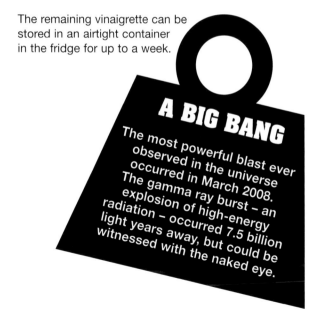

A BIG BANG
The most powerful blast ever observed in the universe occurred in March 2008. The gamma ray burst – an explosion of high-energy radiation – occurred 7.5 billion light years away, but could be witnessed with the naked eye.

MUSHROOM & OXTAIL SOUP

Bovril has been used in soups as a classic flavour-building ingredient for years. Here, we take those flavours to a new height.

SERVES 6

1kg oxtail, trimmed and cut into pieces
2 large onions, sliced
2 large carrots, sliced
2 sticks celery, sliced
2 bay leaves
20 juniper berries, crushed
1 tablespoon Bovril
30g dried mushrooms
500g button mushrooms
sea salt and freshly ground black pepper

Place all the ingredients except the fresh mushrooms in a large casserole or slow cooker.

Cover with boiling water and simmer, covered, on the lowest possible heat preferably in a slow cooker or in a solid fuel stove for 8 hours.

Allow to cool then strain the meat and vegetables from the rich stock. Remove all the bones from the meat, keeping the meat aside, and discard the bones and bay leaves.

In a blender or food processor, strain and reduce the vegetables to a purée with some of the stock and return the purée to a clean saucepan. Add the rest of the oxtail broth, the meat, 600ml of fresh cold water and the button mushrooms, thinly sliced.

Bring to a simmering point and cook for another 15–20 minutes. Check seasoning and adjust if necessary. Serve steaming hot with warm, crusty baguettes.

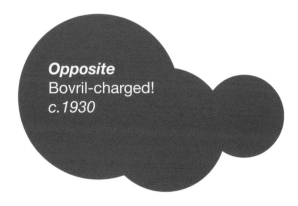

Opposite
Bovril-charged!
c.1930

LITTLE BOVRIL?
That's me!
Just a little
BOVRIL
adds the concentrated
goodness of beef
In bottles—1 oz. 10d · 2 oz. 1/6d · 4 oz. 2/9d · 8 oz. 4/10d · 16 oz. 8/-

CREAM CHEESE, BOVRIL & CHIVE DIP

One of the delightful things about Bovril is just how strongly it can infuse and build flavours. This dip is twice as good once you've added the Bovril.

MAKES ENOUGH FOR 6 TO DIP INTO

200g cream cheese
1 tablespoon smooth peanut butter
1 teaspoon Bovril
2 tablespoons double cream
dash Tabasco sauce
1 tablespoon chopped chives

Simply mix all the ingredients together and serve with a plate of crunchy crudités like batons of raw celery, carrots, sweet peppers, cucumber and florets of cauliflower.

Opposite
Just a little Bovril
c.1950

BOVRIL PRAWNS

It's a fact that when you cook fish you need to add a little salt to bring out the taste of the sea, this sweet and sour dressing to the prawns is rounded perfectly by adding the Bovril.

SERVES 2

500g raw tiger prawns
1 teaspoon Worcestershire sauce
1 tablespoon rice flour
2 tablespoons sunflower oil
2 shallots, finely diced
1 clove garlic, finely diced
2 tablespoons Bovril
2 tablespoons runny honey
1 tablespoon muscovado sugar

Put the prawns into a bowl, drizzle with the Worcestershire sauce and then sprinkle over the rice flour. Toss them a few times to coat.

Heat the oil in a large frying pan or wok, add the coated prawns and stir-fry for 3–4 minutes until the prawns have turned pink. Lift them out with a slotted spoon into a warm dish lined with kitchen paper and keep warm.

Into the same pan add the shallots and garlic and sauté until just golden. Then stir in the Bovril, honey and muscovado and add a splash of water. Bring to the boil, stirring so that everything dissolves, until you have a sauce with a consistency to coat the prawns. Remove from the heat, toss in the prawns, turning them a few times, and serve immediately.

MONO MIGHT

Of all the beguiling athleticism and brute strength within the repertoire of film star and martial arts master, Bruce Lee, his one-inch punch and one-handed two-finger push-ups epitomise the extraordinary conditioning of mind and body of which he was capable.

BOVRIL

Is prepared from **PURE BEEF ONLY**, and is admitted by scientific experts everywhere to be the most perfect form of concentrated nourishment at present known. It contains, besides Peptone, a perceptible powder, which is Albumen and Fibrine, the nutritious constituents of Beef, and by this powder it may be distinguished from clear Beef Tea, which is devoid of staminal properties. **ONE OUNCE** of these constituents contains more real and direct nourishment than **FIFTY OUNCES** of ordinary Meat Extract of Beef Tea. **BOVRIL,** by the simple addition of a spoonful to a cup of boiling water, instantly forms a refreshing, sustaining, and strengthening drink, which has justly been termed a **BOON TO THE AGE.** It is sold everywhere, by the Stores, Chemists, Grocers, and others, in Bottle, Tins, and Lozenges; and is **SERVED HOT** at the leading Hotels, Restaurants, Railway Stations, Temperance Bars, Theatres, and places of Amusement.

SPECIAL NOTICE.

Absolutely purity of everything is guaranteed.

STANLEY RECRUITS HIS STRENGTH WITH BOVRIL

BOVRIL

T. KESSANLY & Cº

HEAD OFFICE: 30 FARRINGDON S

BOVRIL

Is the strengthening article of diet for

ATHLETES ACTORS, SINGERS, AND PUBLIC SPEAKERS.

All speak highly of the advantages derived from such an easily digested and strengthening article of diet as **BOVRIL.** We have number-less testimonials in its favour, which can be inspected at our office. INVALUABLE in the KITCHEN for making SOUPS and enriching SAUCES, GRAVIES, and MADE DISHES.

NO STOCKPOT REQUIRED.

£100 PRIZE

is offered by the Proprietors of **BOVRIL** for the solution of a new and interesting **PUZZLE**, price 3d., or posted to any address in the United Kingdom, on receipt of 4d. in Postage Stamps.

SPECIAL NOTICE.

An eminent public analyst is retained as consulting chemist, and nothing enters or leaves the factory without being examined and tested by him.

EET, E.C.

Stanley's mug
of beef tea
1890

ACKNOWLEDGEMENTS

I've cooked with Bovril since my mother first showed me how to open the jar, sitting on a stool by her kitchen table where I learnt my first culinary skills. I just love the stuff and how it brings flavours together, so thank you, to all behind Bovril, for allowing me the great privilege of writing this book. This book would not have been possible without the endless support and encouragement of Jon Croft, Matt Inwood and Andrea O'Connor at Absolute Press. With that said, the two team members who stood by me through every recipe are my darling wife, Lynda, whose never-ending encouragement saw me through... even when I dropped the pecan pie on the floor, and to my ever-loyal Labrador, Bentley, who kindly helped me clear up the mess.

My huge thanks also go to our friend and associate, Alice Taylor, who has joined the team to work on most of the recipes in this book. Alice: thank you so much.

Finally, to all my friends who have once again sat patiently around our lunch and supper table, tasting and commenting as each dish was developed. Your kind comments were a constant source of inspiration

All Bovril archive images in this book courtesy of the Unilever Archive, except pages 5, 6, 30, 35 and middle picture on page 79, courtesy of Robert Opie, Museum of Brands, Notting Hill, London.

TAKE A TEASPOONFUL OF BOILING WATER

TRADE MARK
FLUID BEEF
BRAND
BOVRIL
SEASONED
BOVRIL LIMITED
LONDON

227g 8oz ℮
Bovril
BEEF AND VEGETABLE
EXTRACTS
BOVRIL LTD · BURTON · ON · TRENT

BEEF
Bovril
THE ORIGINAL BEEF EXTRACT
250g

GLOW
home with
BOVRIL

Long queues . . . wet streets . . . cold winds —
you take them all in your stride when you're
glowing cheerfully after your hot Bovril. Bovril
is concentrated beefy goodness . . . use it to put
beef into meatless meals, too.

The concentrated goodness of Beef

Bovril helps your digestion to get *all* the goodness out of
your food and builds up reserves to resist winter ills.
Bovril stimulates your appetite and your sense of taste.

·IN BOTTLES: 1 oz · 2 oz · 4 oz · 8 oz. and 16 oz.

Glow home!
c.1952